# MEMORIES OF LUTON

*My Life in High Town and Tin Town*
*in the 50's, 60's, and 70's*

By Teresa A. Barker

ISBN 9798358779815

# ACKNOWLEDGEMENTS

I would like to acknowledge and thank the following for assisting me with their knowledge of Luton as well as allowing me the use of their photographs: The Gazette, The Luton News, Hugh Byrne, Kash Farouk, Steve J. Roberts, as well as the Facebook page, "The Luton I Remember." A special thank you goes to Kate McGahan for the invaluable help and guidance she has given to me, allowing me to put my memories into print.

# PRELUDE

I was born in Luton, England as Teresa Leach. I grew up in both High Town and Tin Town, lower income areas in Luton at the time.

High Town was built in the mid to late 1800's. The area consisted of both council and private houses. It was a very vibrant area of town. Our house at 19 Cobden Street was a tiny two-bedroomed council house on the corner of Cobden Street and Taylor Street. With two rooms upstairs and two rooms downstairs, there was no electricity just gas lights lit by an inverted mantle, which I'm told was easily broken and had to be replaced regularly. There was no hot water or inside toilet. There was no heat except for the fireplace. The house must have been very crowded with my mum and dad sleeping in the living room downstairs as their bedroom, and all of the kids in the two bedrooms upstairs. There was even a coffin in one of the bedrooms and the kids had to take turns sleeping in it. Our house, as well as the whole of Cobden Street and other streets in High Town, have since been knocked down. It was a very busy area of town. We were very poor but so were so many others.

*High Town Road - Source: The Luton News*

Tin Town was built around 1946. Prefabricated houses were known as British Steel Framed Houses. They were built as temporary housing due to the housing shortage after the war. There were both council and private houses in this area as well; the top half of each house was made of sheet metal, hence the name Tin Town. The houses came in four different colours: green, blue, salmon pink, and brown. Our house at 41 Burnham Road was green. It was a spacious three-bedroom house with two large bedrooms and one tiny room known as a box room. The house had a front room, a middle room and a kitchen. I didn't know until years later that the middle room was a dining room; it was just known as "the middle room" to us. The house had electricity, hot water, an inside bathroom as well as an outside toilet. The houses were all semi-detached and had very large gardens.

Tin Town consisted of a few roads including Dovehouse Hill, Burnham Road, Williton, Ashcroft, Hartsfield, Yeovil, and Upwell. Over the years many people bought their houses from the council, so they are now mostly private homes. Many have also covered the metal with cladding to give them a completely different look. These houses were meant to be temporary but are still standing strong today.

We eventually moved to 111 High Town Road. This again was a council house known as a two-up two-down house. It was tiny compared to Burnham Road. We had no hot water but we did have electricity. The houses just two doors up still had gas lights. We had an outside toilet and an outside room known as a scullery, which was a room with a sink in it (I have no idea what it was supposed to be used for) and a coal barn. We had no heating, but we had a fireplace in every room. We used to have fires in both rooms downstairs but never lit one upstairs. It was always freezing up there! Our water pipes often froze in the winter. We would have to ask Mr. Williamson in The Welcome Stores opposite us to fill our bucket with water.

*The view of High Town Road from our house.*

Our area was all terraced houses, each which had a passageway shared by four houses. We were lucky to be on the main road where we had every service and business you could ever need. We were very fortunate to have People's Park just around the corner, leading to Pope's Meadow and Wardown Park on the River Lea.

Our house, as well as many others in the area, has since been demolished. There is a school now where my house once stood.

# Table of Contents

# CHAPTER 1

*John & Phyllis – Wedding Day*

I have many memories of my life in High Town, Luton. I will keep all the memories as positive as possible in hopes of not upsetting or embarrassing anyone.

I had the best family ever and wouldn't change a thing. My life started at 19 Cobden Street. My family was my mum Phyllis, my dad John Leech, five sisters: Mary, Pat, Julie, Diane, and Phyllis and two brothers: John and Chris. I was the youngest, my sister Mary was the eldest.

*Phyllis & Chris*

Somewhere along the line the spelling of our surname changed from Leech to Leach. I have no idea why or how this happened, but a couple of the kids are Leech and the rest of us are Leach. My mum died when I was six-months-old, leaving my dad with kids ranging from six months to seventeen years. My sister Mary had to quit her job to help look after the kids.

"MOTHER" AT 17

Looks After A Family Of Eight

*Story from The Luton News*

*Diane (Dinah), Chris, Mary, Phyllis (Till), Julie (Win)*

My mum died on December 10$^{th}$. Just when it looked like there wasn't going to be much of a Christmas at our house, an angel stepped in. There was a knock at the door and it was a big posh car, which turned out to be the mayor's. His chauffeur said an anonymous person wanted to make sure there was a Christmas in our house, being it was such a sad time of the year to have lost our mum. The car was full of toys and goodies which had been sent anonymously by Lady Zia Wernher, who was the residing resident of The Luton Hoo. Lady Wernher was a close friend of Her Majesty the Queen. Her Majesty and her husband, Prince Philip, celebrated their wedding anniversary at The Luton Hoo numerous times, also attending the Sunday morning service at the Parish church. She was obviously a very caring lady.

I was ultimately shipped out to my mum's sister, Ollie, who was a very nice lady. She lived on Yeovil Road in Tin Town. Not long after, my sister Mary married and moved to Canada.

*Tin Town*

My dad and my siblings moved to Burnham Road in Tin Town. This is where my first memory took place. I have no idea of the circumstances but I remember being dropped off at my dad's house. I was about three years old crying, knocking at the door and asking if I could please have a piece of bread. I had on a red siren suit and had wet myself. I remember my legs were all red from the dye. I was taken in and from then on I lived with my family. I would visit my Aunt Ollie on a Sunday, as well as my mum's other sisters, Beryl and Freida. Aunt Ollie always told me that she had a doll for me up in the loft but that I couldn't have it until I was old enough to appreciate it. I never got the doll; I often wonder if it actually existed. We all had our own nicknames that stuck for many years; my dad was Bison, Mary was Lu, Pat was Doe, Julie was Win (after Winnie the Witch), Diane was Dinah, Phyllis was Till, John was Bulls-head, Chris was Buster (after Buster Crabbe), and I was Geezer.

*Diane (Dinah), Chris , Mary, Phyllis (Till), Julie (Win)*

I have many memories from Tin Town. My dad used to go to the pub every night except Sunday when he would get some bottles in; he always used a big green jug. I remember one night I came running into the front room and knocked the whole thing over. That didn't go over too well! I remember my sisters arguing about who's turn it was to stay in with us kids. Then one night the one who was supposed to stay in snuck out, being as my dad never found out. From that night on we were left in my brother John's care.

*On the doorstep in Burnham Rd. Chris, Pat, Teresa, John, Dinah*

One of my happiest and saddest memories was when my sister Pat brought me a nun doll. I loved that doll. Then came harvest festival time at school and we each had to bring something to donate to the Bring and Buy Sale. My nun doll was my only possession so I had no choice but to donate it. I hoped and prayed I would be able to buy it back, but it was on sale for six pence and I only had two. I still love and miss that doll. I have a picture of it from when Pat took me to Hitchen Market one day and we had our pictures taken. I got to hold a monkey that day and she had a parrot on her shoulder.

Pat spoiled me a bit as a kid. She also had a doll's house made for me out of matchsticks. I loved it; it had a door and windows, it was beautiful. One day I came home and it was gone. My dad had sent some stuff to the auction and my doll's house was one of the items. The only toy left was Chris's Noddy bike. I was really upset and so was Pat.

THE DAILY MIRROR

# Snake Gang are proud of 'detective' Pat, 13

By ELIZABETH HICKSON

THE Snake Gang of Cobden-street are not keen on having girls in their ranks. For girls, they believe, are not much good when it comes to trailing imaginary criminals or [illegible] tough jobs of that sort.

[illegible]

But today the gang are proud of Pat. Because last month, on her thirteenth birthday, Pat trailed and caught a real criminal.

[illegible]

## Then She Trailed Him

[illegible]

*Pat featured in The Daily Mirror*

The sisters moved out one by one, eventually leaving me with just my two brothers and my dad.

# CHAPTER 2

While living on Burnham Road (when I was about six or seven), a couple of older kids invited me to go with them to Woolworths, which I did. While there I saw them both steal some items. They told me how easy it was and that I should try it, so I did. I stole a washing line that I was planning on making into two skipping ropes. When I got home I got terrified of what my dad would say so I hid the washing line in the hood of my coat. That said, when I came through the door I must have looked guilty because my sister Diane stopped me. She obviously saw something in my hood. She questioned me about where I had been and where I got the washing line from. She gave me a right telling off and told me I had to return it. I was also not allowed to go anywhere with those girls ever again. I certainly learned my lesson. I have no idea what happened to the washing line.

One time when all of the kids were out playing they said they were going to Woolworth's to get teenage dolls. The dolls were six pence; did I want to go? I said no. I didn't have any money and was too scared to ask my dad as I thought I would know what the answer would be. I'd always been told if you ask you don't get and if you don't ask you don't want. Anyway I thought about it and figured I didn't have anything to lose, so I plucked up my courage and asked my dad if he would give me six pence so I could buy a teenage doll like all the other kids were getting, I was shocked and surprised when he gave it to me! At that moment I thought, "Cor, I must be spoilt. I just asked for something and I got it!" That is the only time in my whole life I asked my dad for anything…and he said yes. I will never forget that.

I never had a bike and to this day I have never driven a bike. I did, however, ride on the handlebars of my friend Shirley's. When I first met her at school

I thought she was really posh, but we soon became really good friends and remained friends until she sadly passed away years later. One day we were riding down one of the side streets in High Town when we crashed at a corner right outside the funeral home. I remember the undertaker came out dressed all in black. He asked in a deep voice, "Are you children okay?" The two of us looked at each other and flew up the road. Luckily we weren't hurt too badly.

*Teresa, John, and Chris in People's Park*

# CHAPTER 3

I remember one night when the electric meter ran out, my brother John had to ride his bike from Burnham Road down to The Freeholders in High Town to get some money from my dad for the meter. He was eleven at the time and had just started Grammar School. Me and my brother Chris, who was eight (I was six) were too scared to sit in the dark so we sat on the wall outside under the lamppost.

We often had a fire in the front room where we burned great big tree trunks. The wood would be in the fireplace stretching right across the room and out of the window. We had to push it through from the outside. I can't remember what we did at the end of the night if it wasn't burnt through. We used the fire to make our toast. We would wait until the bread caught fire, then say, "That's done!" It was usually burnt to a cinder but we thought it tasted good. We used to use the gallon tin of golden syrup that my dad used for his toffee apples as our sugar. I remember spilling it loads of times as it was so heavy for me to lift and then aim it at the cup with my little hands. We would poke the fire with a big pair of black scissors. They were used so much in the fire that they were curled up at the end so that it was a bit of an experience trying to use them as scissors.

# CHAPTER 4

The one time I remember my dad picking me up was when we had a visit from a bloke who had just gotten out of prison. I'd heard my sisters talking, saying he had stabbed a nurse. He started talking to me and I got scared and hung onto my dad. That's the only time I remember him picking me up. I was always scared of my dad, but if he was around I always felt safe.

*This was my Dad, in The Luton News*

Remembrance Day was very special to Dad. I remember standing with him down the town watching the parade. As the soldiers marched by I saw he had tears coming down his face. That's the only time I ever saw him cry.

I remember him chasing my sister Diane up the street with a cat one day. She had done something she shouldn't have and was always terrified of cats. I don't know if he caught her or what happened.

We had a cousin Percy who lived with us for a while. He was a bit of a gypsy but I liked him. He couldn't read but I could, so I remember reading the paper to him. He always mentioned how he loved his Uncle John. Sometimes when he was passing through he'd bring his old gypsy horse with him and tie it up to the back gate.

My sister Pat married Ron who was in the Navy. They lived in Malta and Gibraltar for a while. When they returned to Luton, Pat brought John, Chris, and me reversible jackets with "Malta" on them. We all loved them and wore them with pride.

*Pat and Ron's wedding picture*

# CHAPTER 5

When I was about seven years old we moved back to High Town, number 111 High Town Road. My dad loved it there, as we were virtually opposite The Freeholders. We moved from a three-bedroom house with a bathroom and hot water, into a tiny two-bedroom house. It had electricity but no inside toilet or hot water. We were lucky though, as the houses two doors up still had gaslights. I remember the first night we were there my brother John got up and went downstairs for a drink of water. When he turned the light on we heard a squeal and the floor was covered in beetles! This happened every night when we switched the light on. After a while the council came in and put some powder down. This took care of most of them but we always had a few beetles.

We also had mice. One day I had to warm my dad's dinner up in the oven. I opened the oven door to light it and there were three mice nibbling on his dinner! I immediately jumped up on a chair, and said to myself, "What am I most scared of? The mice? Or my dad if his dinner isn't heated?" So I stomped on the floor to scare the mice and lit the oven. My dad then came into the room and got his dinner out of the oven. He asked me, "How come it's still cold?" So I told him about the mice and he was mad that I would let him eat the dinner the mice were eating. I didn't think he'd mind as every time we got the frying pan out of the tray in the oven it was always full of mice footprints. It wasn't until years later I realized this wasn't normal. I honestly thought everyone had mice footprints in their frying pans.

My dad would give us a couple of pennies in the morning to get some sweets on the way to school. I fondly remember going to Nutter's on Hitchin Road. I loved Tom Thumb Drops because you got lots of them for two ounces. Dad would also pass by the school at lunchtime. I think it was to check that I was in school as I hated school and would often skive off. He would frequently bring a few chocolate eclairs to give to me telling me to share. Of course the other kids soon figured this out and came running – so that lots of times I didn't get one myself.

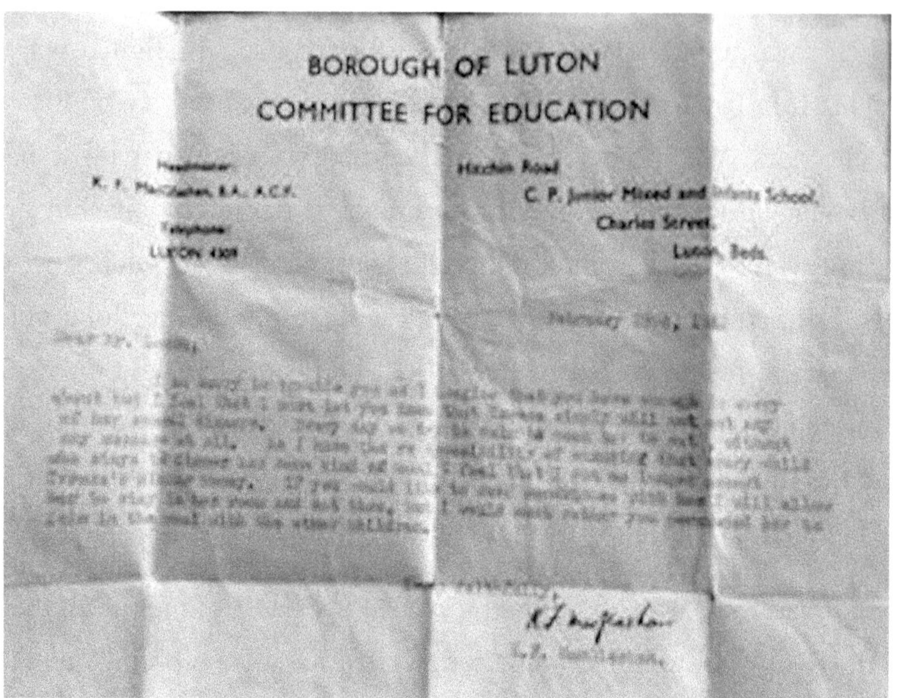
BOROUGH OF LUTON

COMMITTEE FOR EDUCATION

C. P. Junior Mixed and Infants School,
Charles Street,
Luton, Beds.

I got into trouble at school with the school dinners. One day I didn't like the white sauce that was on the fish so I left it, but the teacher who was on duty said I had to sit there until I ate it. I sat there for quite a while. All the other kids were back in class, so I decided I'd better eat it. I did, but immediately threw it back up. My brother Chris was sent to clean it up. We were only seven and nine at the time. After that incident I became too scared to eat any of my school dinners and the headmaster threatened that if I didn't eat them I would get "the cane;" I still didn't eat them. My dad was sent a letter about the situation and it said that I would be allowed to bring a lunch and eat it in the classroom, so from then on I would bring a sauce or sugar sandwich for my lunch. I was locked in the classroom alone but by now I was scared to eat anything at school so I just hid my sandwiches in my desk. Of course after a while they attracted mice, so again my brother was called in to clean my desk out. I'm so glad they can't treat kids like this anymore. One time I remember being starved but too scared to eat my sandwich. The teacher had an open packet of Love Hearts on her desk and I took one. I still feel guilty about that.

# CHAPTER 6

Our toilet was up the backyard. It had no light and had many, many spiders living in there of which I was terrified. I got to know where every spider lived and which one lived in which corner. I would always check who was where before I went in, then I got out as quickly as I could. I remember some of them had big hairy legs, ugh.

We didn't have any hot water or a bathtub so when we had a bath it was round my sister Pat's. We thought we were really posh when we got a bath. Needless to say I didn't get my hair washed very often and was always taken to the side when Nitty Nora came 'round at school. I always had nits and I was sent to the school clinic where they washed our hair in disinfectant stuff. I remember one day at school a classmate asked me if she brought some shampoo in would I wash my hair? That was very embarrassing, but not as much as the time a teacher told me to go wash my neck; she said this in front of the whole class.

I had a very kind teacher who used to call me "Miss Mouse," as I was very shy and quiet. One day she gave me a cardigan that she had knitted. She said she made it for someone in her family but it was too small. I knew she was lying; she just didn't want to embarrass me. It was beautiful and I wore it for years.

*From top left: Mary, Dinah, Till, John, Chris, Teresa*

# CHAPTER 7

*Hitchin Road School. I'm 4th from the left in the front row*

I will always remember when I first started at Hitchin Road Juniors. When Mr. Duncan saw my name he said, "Oh you must be John and Christopher's sister. You sit here at the front." He expected me to be clever like them.

Then I went to Hitchin Road Seniors and when Mrs. Balderstone saw my name she said, "Oh no, please tell me you aren't Phyllis and Diane's sister!" I didn't stand a chance. She proceeded to tell the whole class how Phyllis was naughty the day of the town sports so she was locked in the tuck room while all the other kids were at the sports. When they got back and let her out she had eaten all of the tuck. She always did like chocolate and sweets. Imagine nowadays a kid being locked in a cupboard for hours alone in a school.

The town sports were always a big deal when we were at school. It is amazing to anyone that knows me that I was actually in the town sports. I have never liked PE or sports, but when I was in the Juniors I represented Hitchin Road in the sack race. I felt so proud when we did the Lap of Honour at the beginning of the sports. All the other schools had lots of participants where Hitchin Road only had a very small team. We were also tiny in height compared to the other schools, except for Robert Bohanan. I remember him being tall. I was doing really well until a girl from another school cheated and barged into me, knocking me over. I ended up coming in third.

*Hitchin Rd school team at the Town sports - The Luton News*

# CHAPTER 8

I never liked school and bunked off very often. I was quite clever in some subjects and did well when we had good teachers, but we had quite a few not-so-good teachers too. When it came time to take the 11 plus, I purposely failed. I know most don't believe me but it's true. There was no way I wanted to go to the High School! I saw what happened when both of my brothers went to the grammar school; neither one of them had the proper uniform. I knew the same would be for me, plus I would rather be with the poorer kids than the posh kids. I remember my brother crying because he didn't have an athletics vest. Then my other brother got teased and was embarrassed about how we talked, as my dad talked lots of Cockney. We thought we were talking properly, but when Chris said, "Cor, that's a custy bit of scran," describing his school dinner, the other kids laughed at him saying, "Leach, what are you talking about?"

I actually remember introducing myself as Johnny Leach's dustbin lid. I was often sent to the shop to get peas, pudding, and faggots. I had to take my own bowl and ask for plenty of gippo. It was a long time before I noticed I was the only one taking a bowl and the only one asking for gippo. I would have to go to the butchers to get ten pennies worth of lights for the dog. I didn't know this was unusual…as well as asking for the sheep's head to be smashed in half.

# CHAPTER 9

So off I went to Hitchin Road Seniors on Charles Street, which was all girls. Then in the third year it changed to Stockwood on Cutenhoe Road where we were mixed boys and girls. Also us poor kids were mixed in with the posh kids. The first day I attended Stockwood was the first time I ever remember hearing anyone talking posh. Everyone at Hitchin Road talked the same as me, not cockney but normal Lutonian.

Now I really didn't like school, as I knew I wouldn't. I didn't have the proper uniform; I was missing a blazer and skull cap so I wasn't allowed to go on any school trips or outings. I also had to wear my dad's shirt as my blouse; it was a 17 ½ inch collar and the tails came below my skirt. I was always being told my petticoat was showing when it was the tails of the shirt. Luckily in needlework we had to make our own summer uniform skirt which was navy with red spots. That skirt lasted me till I left school.

I find it funny that at Stockwood –in my last year in needlework– on my report the teacher said I was very slow and showed no interest. I got a C. I find this interesting as after leaving school and to this day I have worked as a seamstress. I thank Eastex for giving me a chance.

Also I was very lucky that my brother John had started work. Our lives rapidly improved because he was very generous in sharing his wages. He gave me the money to buy a swimming costume so that I could do swimming at school. I hated PE. We had one teacher that I really didn't like and one quite nice one. I made myself learn to swim so that I could stay in that nice teacher's class, but the other one I felt was cruel. I was a very tiny girl but she made me attempt thc hurdlcs, throwing the shotput as well as throwing the javelin. Of course I couldn't do any of them. I was sent into the stockroom to get myself a pair of pumps. I had no idea what she was talking about, so I brought out two bike pumps. She thought I was being funny but I really had no idea what she meant. I was then told not to attend PE anymore which of course made me think "YIPPEE!"

I would have loved to have been able to learn an instrument at school and maybe be in the school orchestra, but unless you had an instrument of your own you could only play the triangle, the tambourine, or the castanets. Music has always been my one big passion and I know I would have practiced every day if I had been given the opportunity.

I also had a problem with the school dinners at this school. At Hitchin Road Seniors I loved the dinners, but at Stockwood a new program started where the poor kids could get free dinners. I didn't like how they did it. They first asked who was staying for dinners then they asked who was getting the free dinners. I was too embarrassed to put my hand up as I know others were too, so I got no dinner at all.

I came to realize that a lot of the people I would call "posh" were really nice and I made some really good friends there that I have been in touch with over the years. I loved the other kids; I just didn't like school. I often wonder how everyone's lives have been, luckily with Facebook I have connected with some.

# CHAPTER 10

I certainly think we had the best of times regarding concerts and shows. In Luton we were able to see all of the top entertainers in small venues like The Cali, The Civic, as well as places like The Odeon. Names such as The Beatles, The Small Faces (my favourites), as well as all of the great Motown artists. It's so different today with them mostly performing in huge arenas. In Luton you could actually see the performers instead of them just being a spot, or on a big screen.

Although I never liked school I have always enjoyed writing short stories or poetry. Some of my poems have been known to bring people to tears, usually tears of laughter. Here's a sample. Remember I was twelve when I wrote this, but my sentiments about school are still the same…

SCHOOL

I wake up in the morning and think, Oh No It's School,
Then I realize it's Wednesday and we're going to the pool,
Mrs. Ashby takes us, the waters blue and cold,
It makes us freeze and shiver, but I think that I'll be bold.
From the springboard we do flop and dive
Wondering if we'll all survive.
Then it's time to dry and dress
Oh, I do look an awful mess.
As we walk back to school
We are told not to act the fool

Into the classroom we do file,
The teacher doesn't even smile,
Perhaps she burnt her toast this morning,
Or got up when the day was dawning.
History is a mystery, Math's a bore,
French is a drench, English a chore.
Cookery and Housecraft, that's more like me,
We actually learn what to make for tea.
Games is exercise, running is for sure
Please don't make us do anymore.
In the middle of the morning we feel like our dinner,
Our mothers have told us if we eat less we'll be thinner,
But that doesn't matter
We don't mind if we get fatter .
Here comes our dinner freezing cold
We look at the taters they're full of mould.
Sometimes they're baked and sometimes they're mash
I reckon they all should be thrown in the trash,
Carrots are super, chicken pies are great,
When we have jam tarts they stick to our plate.
Now it's the end of our school day ,
Except for the ones that have to stay,
The bell has gone, hip, hip hooray
But tomorrow is ugh another day.

# CHAPTER 11

My favourite pastimes while growing up were playing two ball and skipping. I'm sure I would've won gold medals in both; I played every minute I could. I also loved comics, mostly The Dandy and Beano. As I got a little older I switched to Bunty, then on to music magazines. I remember when The Beatles came to town a friend asked if I wanted her to get me a ticket. Of course I would've loved to have gone but I didn't have any money. My dad must have felt sorry for me as one day I came home from school and there was a Beatles magazine through the letterbox. He said it wasn't him but I don't know who else it could have been; I loved it. My friend who got the tickets skipped out of school that day, giving the excuse she had to have her eye taken out and cleaned. I don't know if the school believed her but it sounded like a good excuse to me.

One of the best memories I can recall is when my dad came home with a secondhand record player and some old records. I couldn't believe it, there was old Buddy Holly and more! I loved them all and from then on whenever anyone in the house had any money, we bought a record. We had acquired a great collection when one terrible day our house got burgled and the player and all of the records were stolen. The police weren't very nice. They tried to blame my brother saying he did it to collect the insurance money. Of course we didn't have any insurance. We later found out who was behind the break-in and we told the police, but they didn't do anything about it.

I graduated from comics to music papers like New Musical Express and Melody Maker. I would listen to the top 20 every week and I knew the charts by heart. I listened mostly to radio London, radio Caroline or radio Luxembourg. My favourite group of all was The Small Faces. Steve Marriott was and still is my favourite male singer. I saw them when they were in Luton; I also saw them in Wellingborough. I went with my brother and my friend. We caught the train to Northampton but didn't think at the time about how we would get home. It turns out we missed the last train home. My friend and me (we were about 12 or 13) and my brother (two years older), were sitting outside a telephone box when a policeman came along and asked us what we were doing. We told him we'd missed the train. He said we couldn't stay there all night so we had to go with him to the police station. They said we could get some sleep in a cell but we didn't as we were too scared. I was terrified we would be locked up but they said they would put us on a mail train in the morning, which they did. We were met off the train by my dad and my friend's dad. All of us were terrified of what trouble we would be in, but surprisingly neither dad said a word, which made it worse. Turns out both dads had a policeman knock on their doors that morning asking if their children were missing, both feared the worst and thought we'd been murdered. My friend's dad knew she was with me, my dad had no idea where we were. We knew that as long as we were home before he got home from the pub he wouldn't even know we'd been out. I sometimes snuck out, but often would bump into my cousin Reggie. He'd always say "Don't worry, I won't tell your dad." Reggie was a lovely man who tragically died in The Freeholders of a heart attack at age 37.

My favourite film has always been *To Sir With Love.* The school in the film was very similar to Hitchin Road and we had very good teacher at the time that was very much like Sir. He took us all from crayons to perfume!

# CHAPTER 12

Thankfully some things have changed for the better. I remember one time when I had a jumping toothache. I was about nine and I was in agony. My brother John offered to pull it out with a pair of pliers. I was in so much pain I told him to go ahead and do it, but then he wouldn't. We didn't have any painkillers so I just had to put up with it.

Then someone made an appointment for me at the dreaded school dentist. I had never been to a dentist before and had only heard horror stories. My sister Pat took me. I was terrified as all you could hear was kids screaming. I got in there and the dentist said, "Which tooth is it that hurts?" I told him and he then put a gas mask on me and told me to count backwards from 10 to 1. I remember getting to 7.

Another thing we dreaded was the school man. If you weren't in school they would send the school man 'round your house to see why you were absent. A lot of us kids used to bunk off. We would listen for him coming up the road on his moped. As soon as we heard him we would run in and hide. We were scared stiff of him catching us. I have no idea what would have happened if he did. It's kind of like the man in the loft. We were terrified of him too. Some say it was just the wind that made that door move. I don't believe it; I'm sure there's someone up there.

# CHAPTER 13

I loved High Town. It was a great community, where you didn't ever have to leave the street to get anything.

We lived two doors down from Records, the cake shop, which I still think had the best cakes I've ever tasted. They were very kind to us. We would just knock on the door before school and the baker would give us a hot roll and the ladies always gave us extra cakes.

We had The Welcome Stores right opposite. Mr. Williamson there was also very kind. We could go to him to get a bucket of water when our pipes froze, which was quite often. Next to him was Fensom's and Feldman's. Then we had Rigby's, Unwin's, Paula's the hairdresser, and Dunbar's Fish and Fishing, where we would get our maggots and then go to Bedford River on Sunday mornings. We never ever caught a fish. My brothers blamed me for slurping my tomatoes too loud. There was Sinfield's and Stan the Eel Man. I remember one day to show how hot it was, Stan fried an egg on the pavement outside his shop. There was a co-op, a couple of butchers, the café, D E R the telly place, the post office, the bank, the flower shop, the taxi rank, as well as numerous pubs.

We lived closest to The Freeholders and The Painters as well as many other great shops and businesses. These are the ones I used the most. Of course we had the very best fish and chips shop in town. We also had the Launderette. I had to take the washing there on Saturday mornings. I would take it in a bolster pillow case, for it was as big as me. I dragged it down the road like Santa's sack; someone in there usually helped me as I could barely reach high enough to put the money in.

# CHAPTER 14

High Town had many characters when I was growing up, all very nice people. My dad was well-known as The Toffee Apple King because he made the best toffee apples ever! Not that we got to sample many; we got the odd one now and again, but we did get to eat the toffee bits left on the tray.

Family surprise toffee king

*Dad, John, The Toffee Apple King - The Luton News*

Dad had a very hard life with being a soldier in the war, then being widowed when my mum died at age 40. As mentioned, he was left with eight kids aged 6 months to 17 years. He worked as a blocker in the hat factory during the week. On the weekends he worked at the market selling fruits and vegetables with Uncle Les or went round the streets with his barrow or carrier bike selling fruit, vegetables or toffee apples. In his early 50's he lost his leg to diabetes. It all started when he stepped on a piece of wood with a rusty nail sticking out of it. He managed very well with one leg but sadly he ended up losing the other too. He didn't do well after that and passed away at the age of 72.

He was a regular at The Freeholders, but frequented many pubs. He was also a darts champion, winning many cups. He had many friends from The Freeholders and as I said all characters and all very nice people. Most had nicknames. My favourite name was Smut Smith. Then there was Blocky, Big John, Knocker Pates, Wag, Didgle, and Dougle. My favourite couple was Hilda and George Cane. My dad would borrow money from them on a Thursday night so we could all have fish and chips for tea.

My dad had a reputation as being a tough nut; he was tough but not nasty. He had a soft side. He would bring many people home who had nowhere to go, or if they were hungry I'd have to get them a sandwich. He also loved animals. We had chickens and rabbits. I remember a lady and her dog had been hit by a car and killed outside the Freeholders. The lady's husband would lay outside at the place of the accident every night after the pubs closed. Many nights my dad would go sit on the pavement with him.

I was never scared walking at night in High Town. I knew no one local would ever hurt me, plus there was always a policeman in sight or just around the corner. We had a policeman knock on the door one morning when just me and my brother were home. He said, "Excuse me, your chimney is on fire." My brother said, "Thank you" and shut the door. We had no idea what to do so we did nothing. I think we got the chimney swept not long after.

I think High Town had the nicest people I have ever met, a really great community.

# CHAPTER 15

I love Christmas. I can only remember one Christmas at Burnham Road while a couple of my sisters were still living at home. Me, John, and Chris were given a pound each to spend at Evelyn's in Bury Park. It was paid by a provident cheque (I still have no idea what one of those is). I don't remember all that I bought but I know I bought some Christmas cards because I remember my sister Diane looking at what we had chosen. She said I shouldn't be buying cards and what did I plan on doing with them? I had no idea; I just liked the pictures.

I remember Christmas down in High Town. We had a tiny little metal Christmas tree. We named it Spike as it was very prickly. I scratched myself on it many times. My dad had bought it off of someone secondhand. I loved that tree! He would come out every year. I often wonder what happened to him. We would have loads of balloons up as well as paper chains.

We didn't get many presents but we did get some from my older sisters, usually a box of Smarties or something similar. Aunt Doll always brought us something, usually a selection box, which is still my favourite thing to receive. We always had a beautiful fruit display with a few bottles of beer at the ends. We would put it up a few days before Christmas but weren't ever allowed to touch anything until Christmas morning. We would always listen to the Queen's speech. I loved it. The only thing I didn't like about Christmas was the pantomimes on the telly. I couldn't stand them and still can't.

Easter was also special. We would always have fish and chips on Good Friday and fresh hot cross buns from the bakery up the road. As Records wasn't open Easter Sunday, Aunt Doll–as well as my dad's friends George and Hilda–always brought us an Easter egg each. My dad always put them on top of the kitchenette so we couldn't get them, but of course we cheated. Well I know I did. I would sneak bits out of them at the back so it didn't show. By the time Easter came I was lucky if there was anything left in there.

Remembrance Day was also very important, we would always go to the service down the town. I still attend every year when possible.

Halloween wasn't celebrated back then. I was always scared of that night, as I'd been told that's when all the witches and ghosts come out. I liked bonfire night though! We used to make a Guy and go out Penny for the guying. I have no idea where we got the stuff to make the guy. We always had a few fireworks. I liked the pretty ones like the Roman Candle. My brothers used to pick bangers or jumping jacks, which I didn't like at all. We always had a couple of Catherine wheels and rockets but they never seemed to work very well. One year I went to my sister Pat's house and she had indoor fireworks. I'd never seen them before. She also had potatoes in their jackets; very posh!

# CHAPTER 16

There were a few times when we were naughty, but not nasty, or maybe just plain stupid. There was the night just before my dad got home from the pub that my brothers and I decided to give him a scare. We each put tomato sauce all over us and laid on the floor to make it look like we'd been murdered. I can't remember his reaction, but we probably thought it was funny.

Then there was the time Chris had the brilliant idea to get John to sit on an open compass. He set it up between two cushions and said to John "Sit here but don't just sit really plonk down hard," so John did. The poor soul squealed like they do in the cartoons. He pulled it out of himself and flew up and down the stairs 50 thousand times screaming. Chris and I were killing ourselves laughing, It must have really hurt as it was completely stuck in him but none of us checked to see if he needed anything done about it. He should probably have had antibiotics or a tetanus shot at least but he would have been lucky if he had a bit of butter to put on it or a bit of Savlon. I know we never had any plasters or first aid stuff; he just carried on.

One night my dad was just about to sit down to eat his tea when John decided to pull his chair away. Of course Dad went flying. Luckily he didn't get hurt. We were trying to not let him see us laughing but we thought it was very funny.

Chris and I were given the job of painting my dad's barrow. We had a big pot of green paint and had just started painting when I sat on the wrong side of the barrow and tipped it up knocking the pot of paint over onto the grass. I was scared stiff of what my dad would say. I painted it as best I could using the paint off the grass. It of course left a big green patch where it had spilled. Chris then proceeded to tease me when my dad was asking about the paint job. I said yes it was all finished, hoping he wouldn't notice what I had done, by singing it's good to touch the GREEN, GREEN grass of home, emphasizing the GREEN. I don't think my dad ever noticed the extra green grass.

*Dad, John, in the garden in High Town, with his barrow and carrier bike*

My dad did a similar thing with Chris. We often had gypsies coming to the door selling pegs or paper flowers. It was said to be bad luck not to buy from them. My dad would just close the door on them but Chris brought one of their flowers and for quite a while after that my dad would look at Chris and sing PAPER ROSES 🎶

# CHAPTER 17

*Teresa in Tin Town*

As we got a bit older we started to be able to do more stuff. My brothers and I would go to the pictures every now and then. We took turns picking the films. I loved Roman-type films, Charlton Heston type. John liked Doris Day films especially *Calamity Jane* and Chris picked strange films like *Those Magnificent Men in Their Flying Machines (*I remember falling asleep in that one). I remember going with my dad once to see a John Wayne film.

We would also go to watch Luton play. John was football mad, so we sometimes watched the first team, the reserves, and even the youth team. I recall one Boxing Day John was crying because he wanted to go to the football match and we didn't have any money. My dad must have felt sorry for him because he went up to Tin Town with his carrier bike with only figs and dates to sell, but he did it and John was ablc to go to the match. My dad was great on the market;

he could sell anything. He was one of those market people who would shout, "COME ON MY GALS!"

My dad had nicknames for many people. My friend Shirley was "Bins" and my friend Gail was "Blondie." When I was walking to work over the bridge I could tell if one of them was in front of me or behind me when I heard his voice shouting, "WEE-IP BINS!" or "WEE-IP BLONDIE!" He worked at the hat factory that overlooked the bridge.

# CHAPTER 18

As I said we were poor but not the poorest. Our food wasn't the greatest. After my sisters all left home it was just me my dad and my two brothers. My dad did most of the cooking. On Sundays just about everything we had went on the stove at 12 and off at 2, coinciding with the pub hours. Our usual menu was rabbit stew and_sheep's head. I used to have to ask the butcher to break the skull in half and toad in the hole, which was sausages in flour and water (which is glue). We always ate it as that was all there was. Every now and then Aunt Doll would make us a pudding in the basin. I remember one day a friend came over to spend the night. When she asked what we were having for tea, I lifted the lid of the saucepan to reveal a sheep's head and then she said she wasn't hungry. I really didn't realize we had strange dinners, as that's what we were always used to.

I am a terrible cook, as I learned from my dad. When my brother started working our lives improved very much to the point where we would have eggs and bacon on a Sunday and the odd piece of steak which we'd never had before. I remember one day John was cooking bacon on a Sunday morning when my dad, who had a reputation as having bad Sunday moods, told John to keep the bacon quiet; it was too noisy. He then told him to put the thingme in the thingme; poor John tried to keep a straight face and answered, "I'll do whatever you want Dad but I don't know what the thingme is or where you want me to put it."

When my brother Chris started to work our lives got even better, especially mine. My brothers used to have the occasional bet on the horses. If one of them had a winner they had a rule where they would share the winnings. It was called Copstakes. I was lucky to have been included in this even though I didn't bet, so of coursc I lovcd it when they had a winner. Also Chris had Wednesday afternoons off so when I got home from school the washing up was done as well as the fire made. I took care of this the other days. I hated it when I had to chop the wood or the coal if it was in big lumps. It meant I had to go out into the coal barn which I was scared of because of the spiders.

When I started work I thought we were rich! Instead of paying board I would buy the groceries. I would get us a tea every night, like Birdseye beef burgers or fish fingers. I remember my brother John saying to me I shouldn't do that as our stomachs will get used to it and expect something tasty every night. I said, "Well, everyone else seems to get something every night, why shouldn't we?"

One night I had prepared tea and my brother Chris didn't show up to eat it. Of course I got mad and threw it in the bin. When he got home he had his friend Mick with him, who was a cheeky lad. When Chris asked where his tea was, I replied that it was in the bin. Mick smiled looking at the door that happened to have two pheasants hanging on it that my dad was skinning for someone and said something like he thought I'd given his dinner to the birds. It was very funny but I wasn't laughing at the time.

Then it was my turn to go to work. I loved getting a pay packet, I worked at Eastex as a sewer and brought home 4 pounds 17 and six every week. I could finally buy some clothes that actually fit me. When I started the senior school my sisters felt sorry for me because I didn't have a coat. They all put in and bought me a duffle coat. It was miles too big for me but I wore that coat all four years at school from age 11-15. When I first got it, it was down to my ankles and when I left it was like a jacket, but I was very grateful. Just as I was when a classmate's mum knocked on the door with a bag of her daughter's clothes asking if we would be offended if she gave them to me. I was overjoyed. I'd never had such beautiful clothes! At school some of the bullies used to sing "Rag Doll" as I walked by, but not anymore! I had proper clothes!

When I had started work one of my friends brought me a nightdress for my birthday. This was the first nightdress I had ever owned. Now I really did think I was posh.

# CHAPTER 19

*Ken & Teresa in High Town*

When I started dating my boyfriend Ken (who eventually became my husband) my dad asked him if he would give him a lift to pick up some chickens. I told Ken to say no as I knew they would be live chickens and would mess up his car. Ken didn't believe me. He thought I was joking and that they would be frozen. Of course I wasn't joking. They were live chickens and first he had to help catch and then put them in his car. We had a good laugh about that later.

It can be such a small world as Ken was a Tin Town lad. He lived at 35 Dovehouse Hill and I spent my first few years living at 41 Burnham Road. We literally lived the next street over from each other, near enough right in line with each other.

Ken had a couple of experiences at my house in High Town, like when the policeman knocked on the door to say the chimney was on fire. Ken was kind enough to sweep it for us and I was amazed he happened to have a chimney sweep brush.

Another time he had a broken red light on his car, so brain box me came up with the brilliant idea of going to the sweet shop and getting a load of Raspberry Ruffles, as they had the clear red wrappers that we could cellotape together. We sat there munching them as fast as we could, our mouths stuffed to capacity. One of us would say “I can take another,” and this went on until we’d eaten them all. It was only then that someone said why didn’t we just open them and put them in a bowl and just use the wrappers? Neither one of us had thought of that, but at least Raspberry Ruffles are tasty.

# CHAPTER 20

I started dating Ken not too long after leaving school. I was working at Eastex at the time. He had invited me to go to a couple of posh football do's with him. I had never been anywhere posh before! My Eastex friends encouraged me to go so I went to the first one. I got a new dress and for the first time in my life I went to the hairdresser. I had my hair put up and I was extremely nervous all night at the do but made it through okay.

*Ken and Teresa, going to a posh do, the first time I ever went to a hairdresser*

Then came the second one where I was expected to wear a long dress. Of course I never possessed such a dress and certainly didn't have the money to buy one, so I was going to decline the offer. Meanwhile my friends at work got very devious. One of them asked me to be her bridesmaid, which I thought was strange as she hadn't set a date for her wedding. Nonetheless I said yes. She then said she would be making the dresses herself and wanted to make me a paper one to try out the pattern, which she did, I didn't think too much of it until they started nagging me that I should be going to this posh function. I thought it was a bit cruel as they knew I wouldn't be able to get a dress. It was then right after work one day they gathered around my machine and said "Cinderella will go to the ball!" and they presented me with the most beautiful pink long dress that they had all had a hand in making. Of course it fit perfectly because of the paper one. I was completely overwhelmed that they had all been so thoughtful and caring. That was the only long dress I ever owned and I loved it and wore it with pride.

I loved the people I worked with at Eastex, although I didn't like the lift there. It was one of those that had no doors that you had to jump on and off and if you weren't quick enough, you ended up going over the top or under the basement. Fortunately I was young and could easily run up the four flights of stairs, which I did most of the time.

After Eastex I worked at Vauxhall sewing car seats. I hated every minute! I then went to work for Speak Tailoring, a small company that made clothing for Prince Charles. The two tailors worked on his stuff, all hand-sewn and I sewed the copy cats on the machine. They taught me so much. I am forever grateful to them, for that experience led the way for me to be self-employed as a seamstress for the next forty plus years.

# CHAPTER 21

*Teresa & Ken's Wedding*

As I said earlier, we were fortunate to have every service you could think of in High Town. You didn't ever have to cross the bridge for anything if you didn't want to. This was very helpful when I was getting married. I got my cake from Records. It was beautiful! Then there was the catering for the reception from the CO-OP, my wedding cars from the taxi ramp at the end of the road, my flowers from the flower shop…I even had a special bouquet to take to my mum's grave. I know some had concerns that it would be a disaster and I was warned I'd get some dirty old black taxis, but they sent the poshest white cars I'd ever seen. Everything was perfect; I had complete confidence in them all.

We didn't have a photographer as I was very shy and didn't like having my picture taken. I knew my family and friends would take pictures and that was good enough for me. This was the first time I attempted to make a dress. I made mine as well as my bridesmaids. They were all very simple. I actually sewed two inside-out but because of the fabric it didn't show and no one knew except me. We had the reception at Lilly Hall.

We didn't have a honeymoon. We went to The Chicken Kitchen in Westside, which was our favourite, for the American style beef burger.

# CHAPTER 22

Growing up no one really talked much about my mum. We have very few pictures of her. Most people who knew her described her as an angel that was too good for this earth. It sounded like she had had a very hard life. Her husband was sent to fight in the war and at that time she chose to work in the munition factory. She was taking care of all of her kids as well as looking after her mother who had MS.

Mum passed away at the age of 40. My dad had a tobacco tin that had her possessions in it. It contained her rings, the carnation from their wedding and a couple of pressed flowers. We were never allowed to touch this tin, but every now and then I would sneak a peek. He also had what we called "the black box." It was a tin containing different papers. We were told never to touch it. I never did. It kind of scared me, I don't know why. I have no idea what happened to either of these two items that probably hold a lot of our family history.

We were told my grandmother's sister was a passenger on the Titanic and that she was a newlywed. My eldest sister, who had most of the family's history stored in her head, recently passed away so all of that knowledge is now gone. She couldn't remember whether our great aunt survived or not. That's part of the reason I am writing this book, so I can at least give people an idea of the kind of life I had. In all the time since my mum died, us eight kids have never been all together at the same time. We have had a couple of times when there's been seven of us but never all eight. Now of course that can never happen. I really wish I could have known my mum, as well as my grandparents that died before I was born, but I do believe they are with me and are guiding me in my life.

# CHAPTER 23

*My Stockwood Badge*

*My School Picture*

There were many changes in Luton while I was growing up. The biggest one for me was moving from Hitchin Road All Girl's School which was very old and very small. All girls were sent into the brand new Stockwood School on Cutenhoe Road. It was very posh compared to Hitchin Road. It was a mixed school for boys and girls and it had very expansive grounds for cross country running, as well as its own swimming pool, gym, tennis courts, woodworking shop and many other features. There were two four-story buildings and some ground floor buildings. There was some controversy over the fact that it was built at the end of the runway of the airport. If you were on the fourth floor when a plane went over the teacher had to stop talking until it had gone. One thing I liked about Stockwood was that we had our own school orchestra. Oh I would have loved to have been able to be in it but you had to have your own instrument. I did enjoy listening to them.

*Hitchin Road School (above) & Stockwood School (below)*

It is sad to see that Hitchin Road School has now been knocked down and Stockwood is now a different school altogether.

There was also the opening of The International Supermarket. I'd never seen such a big shop! I went there with my brothers; we had never had yogurt before so we bought some chocolate yogurt. It was terrible! We thought that anything with chocolate in it must be good, but that yogurt wasn't. I didn't try yogurt again for many years.

I remember the opening of The Westside Centre, Bury Park. I loved The Chicken Kitchen, especially the American-style beef burger. At lunchtime at Eastex I would either go there, Wimpy for a Wimpy grill, or to British Home Stores for a salmon and cucumber doorstep, which is a six-inch long roll.

Then of course there was the opening of The Arndale Centre, the indoor shopping centre. I loved that place but I must admit I did prefer the outside shops rather than those inside. My favourite was Chelsea Girl where I spent most of my money, as well as Woolworth's, Boots, and Dorothy Perkins. I also enjoyed the market better before it moved into The Arndale. My favourite shop of all was Farmer's Music Shop on Upper George Street where you could go into a booth and listen to any record they had in stock. I also remember going to see The Queen when she opened what was then the new library.

I now live in Vernon, British Columbia, Canada, but Luton and its people will stay in my heart forever. COME ON YOU HATTERS!

<u>A few memorable notations of Luton's rich history</u>

6th Century -The Saxons conquer Bedfordshire

10th Century -Luton has grown into a busy small town

1139-1154 -A castle exists in Luton, giving Castle Street its name

1336 -Luton is badly damaged by a fire

18th Century - Straw hat-making industry booms in Luton

1767 -Luton Hoo is built

1797 -A bridge is built over the River Lee

1801 -Luton's population is 3,095

1834 -Luton gains gas light

1848 -Luton is struck by Cholera

1854 -Luton gains its first newspaper

1858 -the railway reaches Luton

1865 -Luton gains a piped water supply

1872 -Luton gains its first hospital

1876 -Luton is made a borough

1885 -Luton Town FC is founded

1901 -Luton's population is 38, 926

1905 -Vauxhall comes to Luton

1908 -Trams begin to run in Luton

1909 -The first cinema opens in Luton

1919 -Luton Town Hall is burned down during a riot

1931 -Wardown House is made into a museum and art gallery

1932 -Trams cease to operate, they have been replaced with buses

1938 -Luton Airport opens

1939 -Luton and Dunstable hospital opens

World War ll -107 people are killed in Luton by German bombings

1960 -Luton's population is 130,000

1972 -The Arndale Centre is built

1997 -Luton is made a Unitary Authority

1999 -Luton Airport Parkway Station is built

2002 -Car production in Luton ends

2021 -Luton's population is 225,300

*Photo Credit: Hugh Byrne*

# ABOUT THE AUTHOR

Teresa Barker grew up in Luton England, later emigrating to Vernon British Columbia Canada where she now lives with her husband Ken and her Afghan Hound, Roxey. She felt compelled to write this book to give people an idea of what life was like for her in Luton in the 1950s, 60s, and 70s. This is the second book to be written by this author, the first being "The Twelve Trees of Christmas."

Teresa can be reached via email at **teresab6@shaw.ca**

www.ingramcontent.com/pod-product-compliance
Lightning Source LLC
LaVergne TN
LVHW080458160826
845677LV00006B/1397

* 9 7 9 8 3 5 8 7 7 9 8 1 5 *